McGRATH MATH

TEDDY BEAR
ADDITION

Barbara Barbieri McGrath

Illustrated by **Tim Nihoff**

Charlesbridge

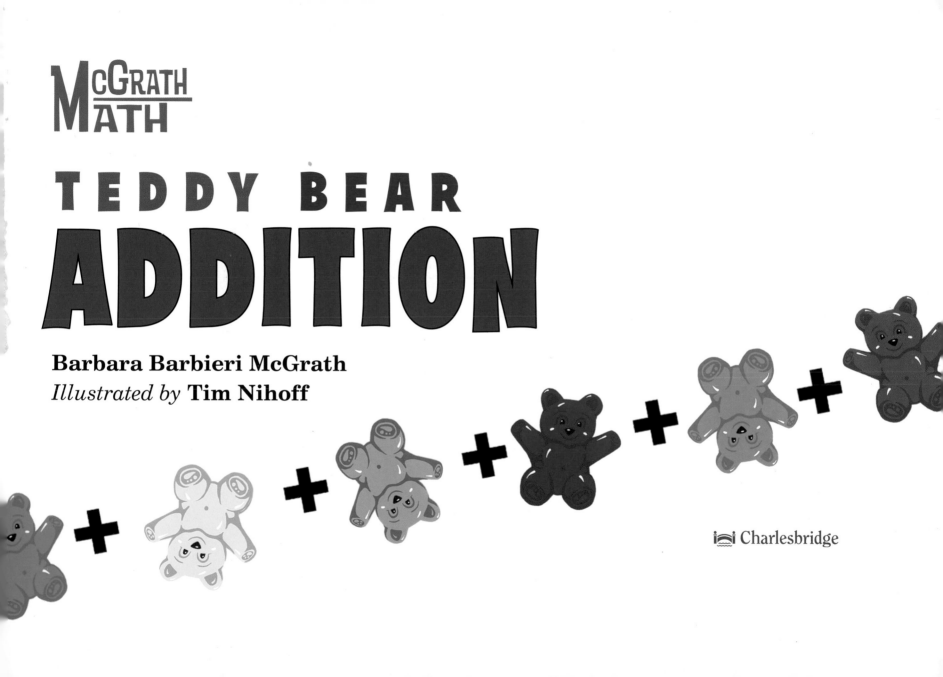

Published by Charlesbridge
85 Main Street
Watertown, MA 02472
(617) 926-0329
www.charlesbridge.com

Library of Congress Cataloging-in-Publication Data
McGrath, Barbara Barbieri, 1954–
   Teddy bear addition / Barbara Barbieri McGrath ; illustrated by Tim Nihoff.
     p. cm
   ISBN 978-1-58089-424-1 (reinforced for library use)
   ISBN 978-1-58089-425-8 (softcover)
   ISBN 978-1-60734-633-3 (ebook)
1. Addition—Juvenile literature. I. Nihoff, Tim, illustrator. II. Title.
QA115.M388 2014
513.2'11—dc23   2012038696

Printed in Singapore
(hc) 10 9 8 7 6 5 4 3 2 1
(sc) 10 9 8 7 6 5 4 3 2 1

Illustrations hand drawn digitally and collaged with
   found objects in Adobe Photoshop
Display type set in Animated Gothic by BA Graphics
Text type set in Century Schoolbook by Monotype
Equations type set in Billy by SparkyType
Color separations by KHL Chroma Graphics, Singapore
Printed and bound September 2013 by Imago in Singapore
Production supervision by Brian G. Walker
Designed by Whitney Leader-Picone

With love to my lifelong "playmate," Joyce—B. B. M.

With love to my A+ big brother, Rob—T. N.

A big teddy welcome
from math-loving bears.

Let's count, add, and play
without any cares.

Pour out the teddies
to add the bear way.
First guess how many
are ready to play.

Guessing how many is called "guesstimating." It's fun because there is no wrong answer.

To find out the answer
about the amount,
line up the teddies
and count, count, count!

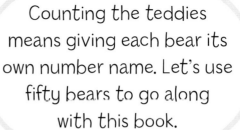

Counting the teddies means giving each bear its own number name. Let's use fifty bears to go along with this book.

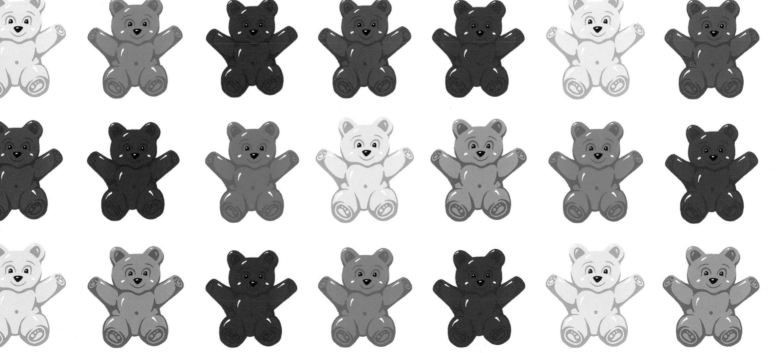

Sort teddies by color.

Call each group a set.

Count each different color.

What did you get?

13

orange
set

7

4

blue
set

red set

yellow set

10

purple set

5

green set

11

There are many ways to sort.
Here we are sorting bears by color.
Just by looking, you can probably
tell which color has the most bears.
Count the bears in each set and
write that number down.

Put the sets together.
No group is the same,
but the numbers you combine
share a special name.

The numbers you add
are called addends.

5

4

addend

addend

Purple plus blue—
teddies are having a ball.
Find the total, or sum,
by adding them all!

There are five purple
bears and four blue bears.
When you put the two colors
together and then count
them, there will be nine bears.
The total is called the sum.

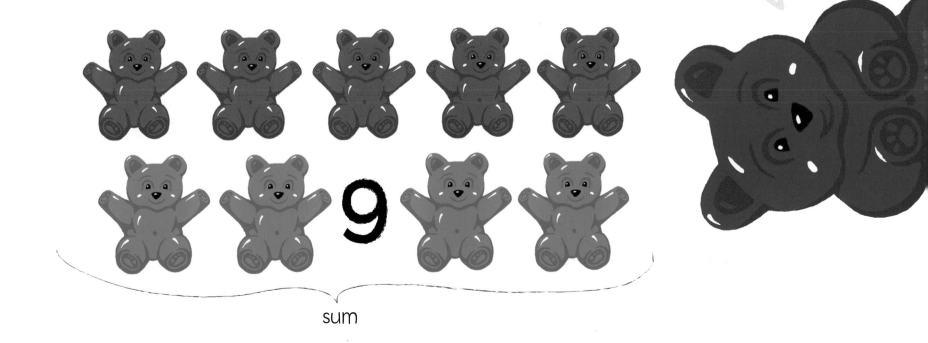

9

sum

Let's write an equation.
The sum is still found.

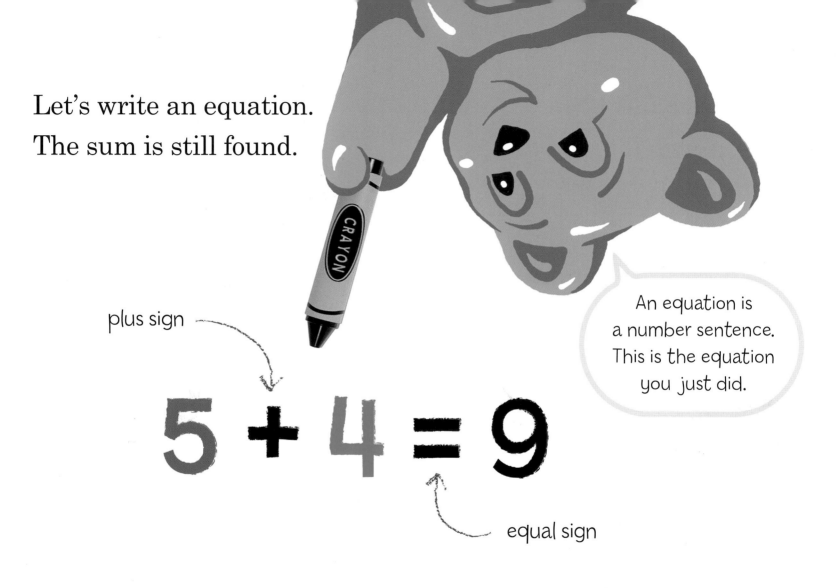

plus sign

An equation is
a number sentence.
This is the equation
you just did.

5 + 4 = 9

equal sign

The bears don't get dizzy
when you turn it around.

The plus sign means add.
It goes between the two numbers
you want to add. The numbers on
each side of the equal sign must
have the same value. Equations
can also be reversed.

$$9 = 4 + 5$$

reversed equation

Look at this equation.
Does it seem rather tall?
Addition can be vertical—
it's no trouble at all!

You can also put the numerals on top of each other, like this.

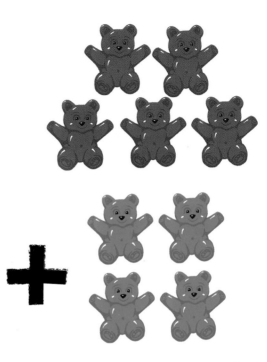

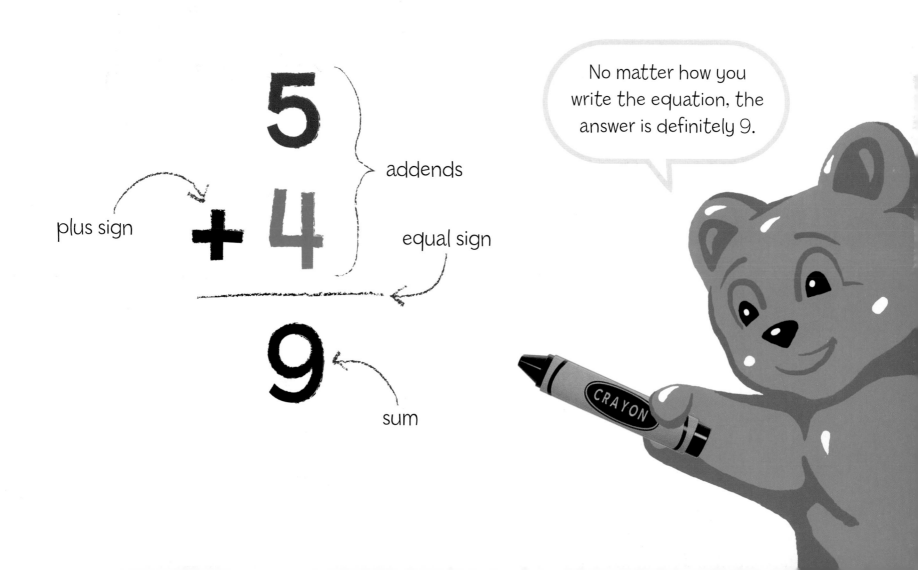

All numbers have value,
a fact we must face.

digits

0 1 2 3 4 5 6 7 8 9

The numbers
0 through 9 are
called digits.

Put them in columns.

Show them their place.

Bigger numbers, from 10 to 99, use two digits: one digit in the ones column and one digit in the tens column.

tens column

1 2

ones column

CRAYON

Bigger bear numbers
want in on the fun.
Complete the equation—
get two digits, not one.

7 + 4 = 11

Add the orange and blue bears together, and you will get a two-digit number. Digits can have different values depending on their place in the number.

In the tens column the 1 has a value of 10, or one ten.

In the ones column the 1 has a value of 1, or one one.

Yellow plus purple.
Red teddies plus blue.
Green bears plus orange.
Each sum will be new.

Let's practice adding!

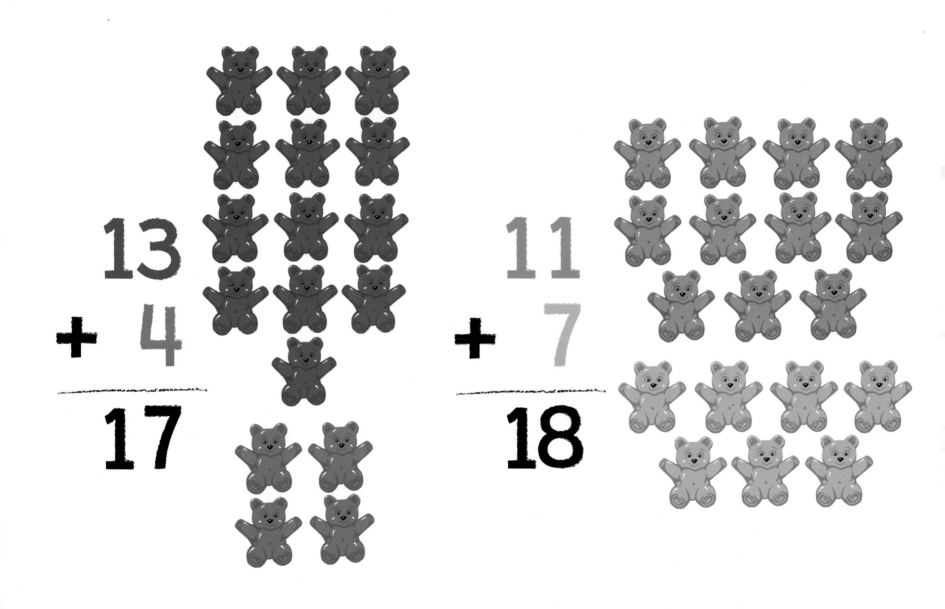

13
+ 4
―――
17

11
+ 7
―――
18

Adding two-digit numbers
will mean even more.

Watch what happens
when we add the green and
yellow bears together!

Higher and higher
the numbers will soar!

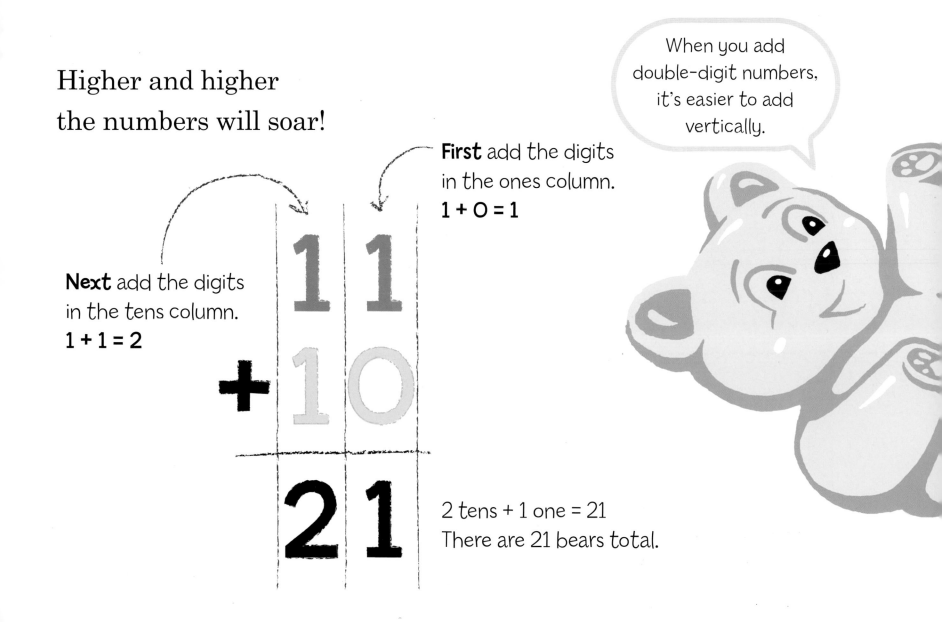

First add the digits
in the ones column.
1 + 0 = 1

When you add
double-digit numbers,
it's easier to add
vertically.

Next add the digits
in the tens column.
1 + 1 = 2

1 1
+ 1 0
———
2 1

2 tens + 1 one = 21
There are 21 bears total.

To add four sets of teddies,
add the groups two by two.

Then add the two sums.

How did you do?

$$\begin{array}{r} 23 \\ +15 \\ \hline 38 \end{array}$$

To add bigger numbers,
take a breath—don't get tense.

Let's add all the color sets together. Set up your number columns.

1. Add the numbers in the ones column. They add up to 20. That simply doesn't fit! The 2 in the 20 must get over to the tens column.

2. Carry the 2 and place it in the tens column. The tens column has 3 tens already.

3. Add the numbers in the tens column. There are 5 tens total.

So the answer is 50.

2

13
11
10
7
5
+ 4
——
50

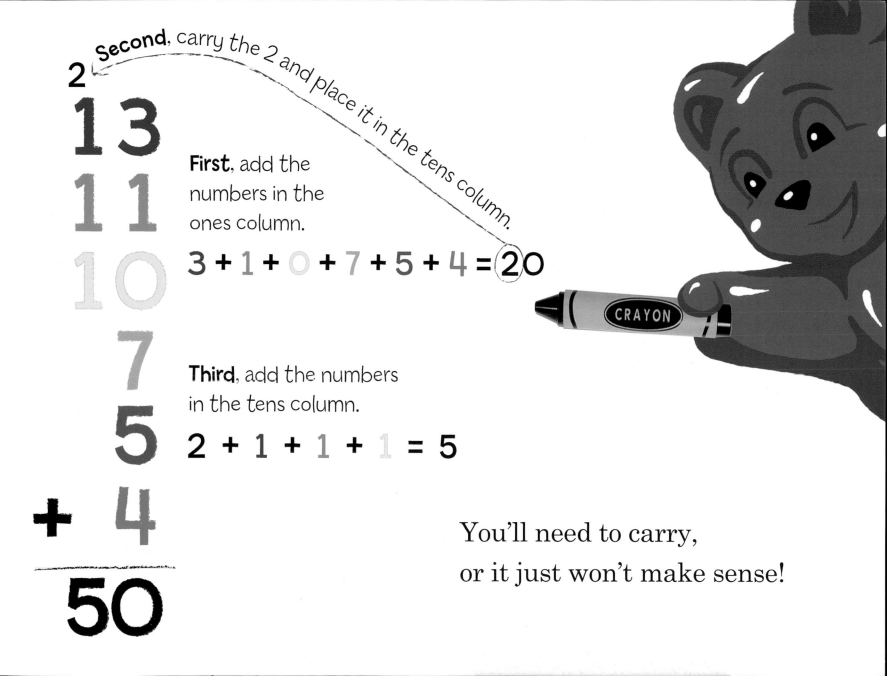

Second, carry the 2 and place it in the tens column.

First, add the numbers in the ones column.

$3 + 1 + 0 + 7 + 5 + 4 = 20$

Third, add the numbers in the tens column.

$2 + 1 + 1 + 1 = 5$

You'll need to carry,
or it just won't make sense!

Addition was fun,
but there is a way
the bears in this book
can be taken away.

It's called
subtraction!

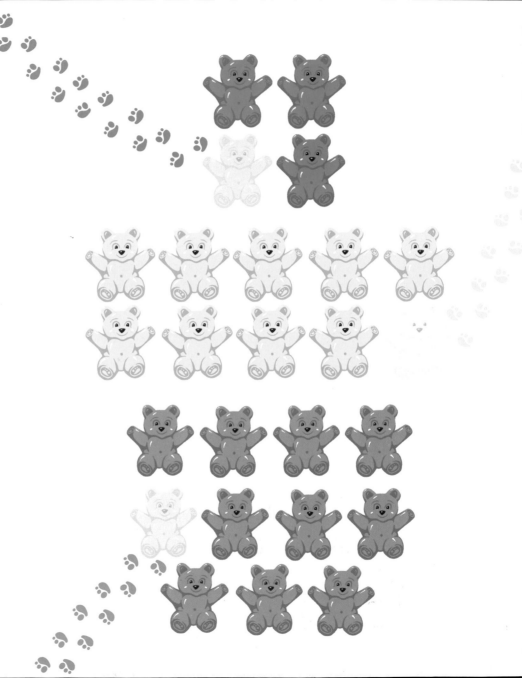

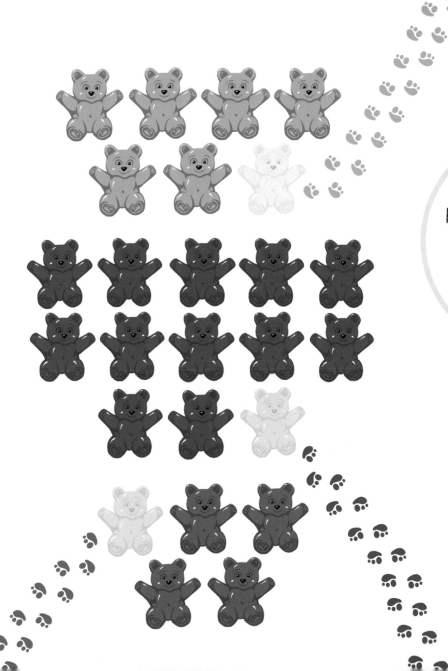

With addition, you add to get a sum. Adding teddies is great because you get more. With subtraction, you take away to find what's called the difference. It's a perfect way to put the bears back to get ready for more learning fun!

You've done teddy addition, but before you subtract,
a review helps you remember—and that's a bear fact.

GUESSTIMATING AND SORTING

DOUBLE-DIGIT ADDITION

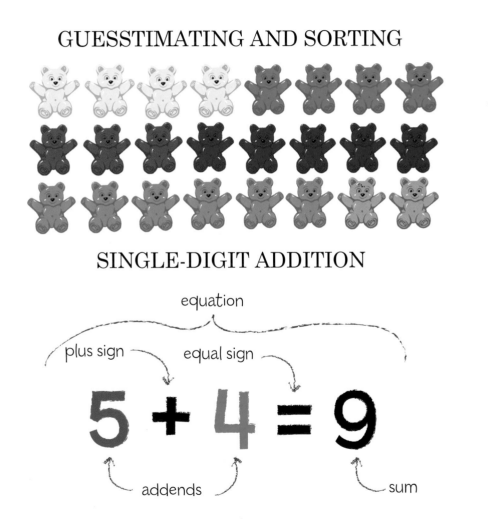

SINGLE-DIGIT ADDITION

equation

plus sign — equal sign —

5 + 4 = 9

addends — sum

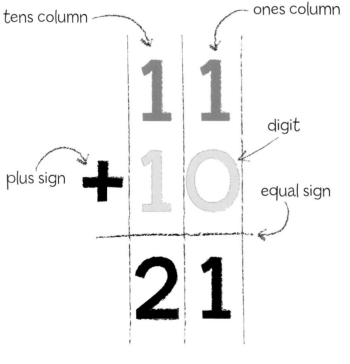

tens column — ones column

digit

plus sign +

equal sign

1 1
1 0

2 1